The Body Boundaries Parenting Guide

The
BODY
Boundaries

Parenting Guide

Eight Essential
Body Safety Conversations
to Have with Your Kids

Julie Bemerer, PsyD

Zeitgeist · New York

To my village

Zeitgeist™
An imprint and division of Penguin Random House LLC
1745 Broadway, New York, NY 10019
zeitgeistpublishing.com
penguinrandomhouse.com

ISBN: 9780593885994
Ebook ISBN: 9780593885932

Illustrations by Clarice Diamantino
Book design by Katy Brown
Author photograph © by Sara Simonson
Edited by Sarah Curley

Printed in the United States of America
1st Printing

The authorized representative in the EU for product safety and compliance is Penguin Random House Ireland, Morrison Chambers, 32 Nassau Street, Dublin D02 YH68, Ireland. https://eu-contact.penguin.ie

Contents

INTRODUCTION

It's Never Too Early to Teach Your Child About Body Safety

Children are like sponges, soaking up the world around them. They often comprehend more than we realize, which is why we can introduce them to concepts of body boundaries and consent at an earlier age than we might expect. Once a child is able to express preferences, that's a great time to start these conversations, which we can continue and build on throughout childhood and adolescence. You've probably noticed that, even from infancy, your child showed curiosity about their body. As they grow to explore, discover, and question how their body works, we, as caregivers, can use those discoveries as opportunities to teach about body safety.

As caregivers, we want our children to be empowered to understand body safety rules, how to set boundaries when they feel uncomfortable, and how to respect other people's boundaries. We can think of "body boundaries" as limits we set for others regarding how they look at or touch our body or enter our personal space. "Consent" occurs when we explicitly tell someone they can enter our personal space or do an activity with us. Children begin to learn about body safety by watching their caregivers interact with them and others, but it's equally important to supplement these observations with purposeful conversations.

This book is a guide for caregivers to introduce and discuss these topics with young children. In these pages, I provide recommendations for age-appropriate conversations that will educate and empower your child, not scare them. As you discuss these concepts with your child, be prepared for any awkward or uncomfortable feelings you may have. Perhaps you grew up in a family that didn't discuss these topics. Take some deep breaths, and laugh along the way if it helps. By making these topics and activities fun for your child, you'll keep them engaged and help them learn. It's okay to laugh together, even when discussing serious topics.

This book is not a comprehensive guide to the many conversations you will have with your child, but it's a start in a positive direction and can promote an atmosphere of openness in which your child feels comfortable talking with you about difficult subjects. As your child grows, you can build on this foundation, so, by the time they are an adult, they have a full understanding of boundaries and consent and how to assert them and identify them in others.

As a clinical psychologist, I specialize in working with children who have been traumatized, particularly by child abuse. I am passionate about providing children body safety education while they are young to prevent child abuse. My goal is to provide a step-by-step guide for helping your child understand these topics and feel comfortable sharing with you about any topic, including these more difficult ones. I have guided many caregivers in having this conversation with their children. I feel confident this book will provide the tools you need; however, most pediatricians and therapists can help guide you if you need additional help. You did the right thing by picking up this book—it shows how invested you are in your child's well-being and their future. By talking to your child about body safety, your child will be more confident, self-assured, and respectful, which will benefit them for their entire lifetime.

FOLLOWING THE LEADER

As caregivers, we're the leaders in setting and enforcing clear boundaries for our children and ourselves. Children mimic the behaviors they see. Who are your children around, and who do they trust the most? You! By showing them how you respectfully interact with them and others, your child will acquire those strategies. When your child throws a tantrum, model for them how to create a safe space so no one gets hurt. When someone raises their voice, model how to clearly tell that person to stop or you will walk away. When you tickle your child and they say stop, respect their boundaries by immediately stopping. Similarly, if your child is climbing on your head, tell them to stop, and model how to get someone out of your personal space in a respectful way. If they don't comply, model how you get up and move away or choose an alternative consequence for ignoring your boundary.

PREPARING TO TALK WITH YOUR CHILD

Most topics don't need to be discussed with your child in a formal sit-down talk. You can introduce these topics as everyday examples arise. Many activities in this book can be woven into regular playtime throughout the day. You might also choose to initiate some of these talks during a car ride or a walk, when there is less pressure on the child to engage directly by maintaining eye contact or sitting still.

When using the scripts and activities I provide, feel free to adjust the age appropriateness of the topic or the words you choose depending on your child's verbal and comprehension abilities. By using straightforward language and keeping conversations short—ideally, 5 to 10 minutes—you'll help them stay more focused and remember what you said. Repetition over time will help this information stick.

HOW TO USE THIS BOOK

Each chapter introduces a new topic about boundaries. You'll get an overview of the subject, an explanation of new vocabulary, and an interactive section that includes a conversation guide, three sample scripts, and four activities to engage and teach your child. The sample scripts will give you an idea of how to introduce the topics. Your child's response will help you build on the topic. You don't have to say the script word for word but rather hit the main points as your child responds and asks questions.

The chapters are meant to build on one another, so you'll get the most from this book if you go in order. However, don't feel as though you must complete every activity. There may be activities you decide to sprinkle in over time as your child gets older.

For best results, work through the book slowly—ideally, no more than one chapter every week or two, and keep these interactions short. Days or even weeks may go by without one of these conversations—and that's okay. You know your child best, so do what works for your child and lifestyle.

CHAPTER 1

Listening to Your Feelings

TEACHING YOUR CHILD to identify their feelings or emotions is a great place to start because this skill helps them get in tune with their body. Even at a young age, children can begin to identify the four basic feelings: happy, sad, angry (mad), and scared. When they can identify and name their feelings, they can begin to understand how feelings help them and how to better control their body when strong feelings occur.

WHY THIS, WHY NOW?

Feelings can be useful—even uncomfortable feelings—because they help inform us that we need to seek safety. Without the ability to feel scared, we might not look both ways before crossing the street. Without feeling anger, we might not defend ourselves against someone who is hurting us. If you teach your child about listening to their body and identifying their feelings, they will begin to understand the "gut feeling" concept, a valuable tool for keeping safe.

Vocabulary

- If you haven't already, begin teaching your child the four basic feelings or emotions: **happy**, **sad**, **angry (mad)**, and **scared**. Look for opportunities to use these words, such as, "You look so happy to see Grandma!" or, "With that frown, it looks like you're sad that it's bedtime. Let's read a book."

- Add the word "**upset**" to describe sad, mad, and scared feelings as children learn to distinguish between these feelings. It's a nice vocabulary word when they don't want to share details about or aren't sure of their feelings but need to communicate what they need in the moment. They can just say, "I'm feeling upset."

- Over time, add the word "**uncomfortable**" as you teach them about how upsetting feelings make their body feel.

It's almost never too early to begin these important lessons about feelings. Studies have shown that infants are able to read other people's feelings and that toddlers can begin naming their feelings as their language develops. Just like you taught your toddler to say yes and no, you can teach your child feeling words. As they grow older, add more complex emotions, such as annoyed, excited, surprised, and more, helping them make connections between the word and the feelings in their body.

CONVERSATION GUIDE

Let's start the conversation about feelings. While these conversations are a great start to a child's education in body boundaries, there's an added bonus: By talking with your child about feelings, they will become more comfortable sharing their feelings with you and more likely to share increasingly difficult feelings as they grow older.

GETTING STARTED

What better place to start than by teaching your child that everyone has feelings? Name some people they love, and share how they each have feelings. From there, start teaching them about the four basic feelings.

Try to help your child make connections between the feeling word and the feelings they are having in their body. When they're happy, tell them how their smile or laugh lets you know they're happy. When they're mad, describe what you see, such as making fists or turning red.

CONTINUING THE CONVERSATION

As your child starts to understand the basic feelings and how they can notice them in their body, add additional feeling words to their vocabulary by labeling the feeling as they feel and express it. If they can't put a toy together easily, you can teach them about feeling "frustrated," another feeling word in the mad category. When their friend can't come over, you can teach them "disappointed," another feeling word in the sad category. Help them read their body's clues, and connect those to situations they may find themselves in. After meeting a stranger, you might ask your child if their body gave clues that they were feeling a certain way. Share how feelings like this keep them safe from talking to or getting close to strangers.

Your child might not always know how they are feeling, and this is okay. Reassure them, and let them know you're there to help as they try to work through different feelings. There are also times in life when more than one feeling comes up at once. When this happens, help them sort out why they feel this way.

SCRIPTS

Here are three scripts you can use to talk with your child about feelings. Script 1 is geared toward a three-year-old, script 2 to a four- or five-year-old, and script 3 to a six-year-old. Feel free to adapt these to meet your child where they are.

SCRIPT 1: WE ALL HAVE FEELINGS

Caregiver: I love playing dolls with you. Sometimes, the dolls cry because they need something. We all have feelings. Did you know that?

Child: M-hm. Can I have that doll?

Caregiver: Sure! I have feelings. Grandpa has feelings. Auntie has feelings. Even you do!

Child: I like you.

Caregiver: It sounds like you are feeling happy while we play together. I feel happy right now, too. That's why we're smiling.

Child: (Hugs caregiver.)

Caregiver: We also have feelings that don't always feel good, like mad, sad, and scared. Those feelings are okay, too.

Child: Dolly is sad. She wants you to hold her.

Caregiver: Great job noticing she is sad. I will hold her so she feels better. I love helping you feel better, too.

SCRIPT 2: FEELINGS REVIEW: RIDING IN THE CAR TOGETHER

Caregiver: Do you remember who has feelings?

Child: Everyone!

Caregiver: That's right. Tell me about a time you were happy.

Child: When we got ice cream yesterday. I liked that all our family was there.

Caregiver: Oh, I felt happy then, too. I remember we were all smiling and laughing. My heart felt so much love. Tell me about a time when you felt sad.

Child: Hmm, I don't know.

Caregiver: I remember one time you were frowning and crying after you said goodbye to Grandma when she got on the airplane.

Child: I miss Grandma.

Caregiver: When we miss people, we feel sad. That's right. When did you feel mad?

Child: When Sissy took my toy. She always takes my stuff. I don't like it.

Caregiver: Yes, when we get mad, it's usually because we don't like how someone is treating us. That means we need to get help dealing with that person.

Child: Yeah, you got my toy back for me.

Caregiver: That's right. I'm here to help you and your sister with your feelings, especially the upsetting ones.

SCRIPT 3: MAD FEELINGS

Caregiver: It looks like you are mad because your brother pushed you out of his way. Your muscles got tight, and you had a burst of energy, which tells me you are mad.

Child: He makes me so mad!

Caregiver: I know. That mad feeling told you he did something you didn't like. You didn't like that he hurt you.

Child: Yeah, he's so mean.

Caregiver: Mad helps us stay safe. When he pushes you, I want you to get away from him so you don't get hurt again.

Child: I just get so mad!

Caregiver: I know. As soon as you get that mad, run out of the room so you don't hurt anyone. Can you give it a try?

Child: Okay (runs out of room, then returns).

Caregiver: I'm proud of you for trying that strategy. Come find me next time you're mad. I will help you. Now, I will speak to your brother about his behavior.

ACTIVITIES

Here are four activities you can weave into your interactions with your child to help teach and reinforce information about feelings. You might pick one activity to do now, and do additional activities as your child gets older, or repeat activities as you'd like, making them more age appropriate as your child grows.

Feeling Identification

We've talked about naming your child's feelings as they are happening and having conversations about feelings. This activity can also help them understand other people's feelings.

Understanding other people's feelings is a skill that will help your child identify situations that require boundaries as they get older.

MATERIALS
· Paper
· Crayon or marker (optional)

INSTRUCTIONS
1. Down the left side of the paper, draw a happy, sad, mad, and scared face.
2. Down the right side, in random order, draw pictures of situations that might cause those feelings (see note following).
3. Discuss the four feelings with your child.
4. Ask your child how each situation would feel.
5. Draw a line from each situation to the corresponding face.

NOTE: Here are some ideas to get you started:
· Receiving a gift
· Hearing a loud noise
· Someone taking their toy
· Saying goodbye to a friend

During this activity, help your child make connections between these feelings and the times they've experienced them. As your child gets older, add more complicated feelings, such as frustrated, disappointed, confused, and embarrassed, or add situations where two simultaneous feelings may apply. Throughout the activity, praise them with comments like, "I love talking about feelings with you" or, "I'm proud of you for talking about upsetting feelings with me."

Feelings Charades

Feelings Charades is a fun and silly way to get your child comfortable talking about their feelings. It will also help them learn to read other people's faces and understand how they might be feeling. For example, if they can see that someone looks angry, they will be able to give that person space, which will help them stay safe from hurting touches.

As you guess your child's feelings, share the clues that show how they are feeling, such as, "You are happy. I can tell by your smile" or, "I think you are sad because you're looking down and frowning."

MATERIALS
- Pictures of facial expressions for ideas (optional)

INSTRUCTIONS
1. Tell your child you're going to make a face and you want them to guess which feeling it shows.
2. Make a feeling face. Offer clues until they identify the feeling.
3. Next, let your child make a feeling face and guess the feeling they're showing.
4. Take turns making faces and guessing.

NOTE: Praise your child for identifying the feeling correctly, and offer reassurance if they get stumped. Talk about the clues our face and body give with different feelings.

Feelings in the Body

Our body gives us clues to our feelings, but not every clue can be seen on our face. When we are happy, we might smile and feel lightness in our chest. When we are angry, we might make fists with our hands or notice our heart beating faster. When we are sad, we may cry, frown, or feel heavy in our chest. And when scared, our muscles tighten and our stomach might hurt.

This activity will help your child get in tune with their body's clues in response to different feelings. As they make the connection between their feelings and their body's clues, your child will learn how to listen to their body in potentially unsafe situations. This way, they will know when to leave a space or get help.

MATERIALS
- Paper
- 4 different-colored crayons or markers

INSTRUCTIONS
1. Draw an outline of a body on a piece of paper.
2. Let your child choose which color they want for each feeling—happy, sad, mad, and scared.
3. Name a feeling, then ask your child where they notice that feeling in their body.
4. Circle or color those parts with the assigned color.
5. Repeat for each feeling.

NOTE: Ask your child if they have ever noticed what happens first in their body when they are upset. This can help them identify their feelings as soon as they arise. If your child has a hard time identifying where they feel clues, tell or show them where you notice it inside yourself.

Safe and Unsafe Situations

When your child learns to identify safe and unsafe situations, the stage is set for them to get help as needed.

Having this conversation helps your child become comfortable talking about difficult or scary things. Common safe situations might include family movie nights, going to the store together, sharing toys with friends, watching adults laugh together, or listening to a teacher read a book to the class. Common unsafe situations might include seeing a fire inside, being spoken to by a stranger without a caregiver present, watching someone take a toy from someone else, being hit by another child, or hearing adults yell.

MATERIALS

- Paper
- Crayon or marker

INSTRUCTIONS

1. Draw or write three safe situations and three unsafe situations on the paper.
2. If drawn, ask your child to circle the safe situations and cross out the unsafe ones. If written, describe each situation and invite your child to say "safe" or "not safe" in response.

NOTE: Provide reassurance by pointing out all the people in your family and community who help with unsafe situations. Praise your child for being honest and open with you. End the activity on a positive note and even a hug to decrease any related anxiety, and help them get back to their regular routine. As children get older, revisit this activity, adding new age-appropriate situations.

CHAPTER 2

Learning About Boundaries

THIS CHAPTER FOCUSES on teaching your child about body boundaries and personal space. Body boundaries are limits we set for others regarding how they look at or touch our body or enter our personal space. By coaching your child during and after real-life boundary violations, you will help them understand what their boundaries are and how they can protect their boundaries in difficult situations. Similarly, teaching them how to avoid touching others in unwanted or hurtful ways introduces them to the social skill of respecting others.

WHY THIS, WHY NOW?

By age three, children can begin to understand okay and not-okay touches and personal space. If your child spends time with others, attends childcare or preschool, or complains about another child hurting them or looking at them when they are getting dressed or bathing, it's a great time to introduce these topics.

Vocabulary

Terms like "**okay**" and "**not-okay**" touches or "**safe**" and "**unsafe**" touches help children understand different types of touches. It's not recommended to use "**good**" and "**bad**" in reference to touch, as those words include judgment. If they consider them "bad," they may not want to tell you because, to them, "bad" implies they will be in trouble or that they are bad.

CONVERSATION GUIDE

By teaching your child about body boundaries, you will help them understand and respond when someone violates their boundaries, how to respect other people's boundaries, and how to keep their body safe. Hurting touches are common among young children, which makes them a good introduction to creating boundaries.

GETTING STARTED

Real-life opportunities can get this conversation started. If another child pushes your child on the playground or their cousin hits them, label it a not-okay touch. When your child gives you a hug or high fives their friend, label it an okay touch. By labeling touches, your child will begin to develop categories in their mind. After labeling the touch, you can talk more about okay and not-okay touches to help your child understand everyone has boundaries and personal space we need to respect.

CONTINUING THE CONVERSATION

As your child begins to understand the difference between okay and not-okay touches, continue to coach them in everyday situations. To help your child grasp the concept of personal space, discuss that we all have a "bubble space" around us. Bubbles can be different sizes at different times. Show your child how their bubble might be small around you but large around a stranger. Using real bubbles, you can help them see what happens when two bubbles collide and burst. This visual example illustrates why we all need to respect personal space. As your child gets older, they can begin to understand nuances in personal space, for example, that it's not okay when someone steps into their personal space without permission but is not physically touching them.

This conversation introduces several important life skills. By learning to listen and respond to others' needs as well as their own, your child will build confidence, conviction in their boundaries, attunement to the personal space needs of others, and trust and respect in their relationships.

SCRIPTS

Here are three scripts you can use to discuss boundaries. Script 1 is geared toward a three-year-old, script 2 to a four- or five-year-old, and script 3 to a six-year-old. Feel free to adapt these to meet your child where they are.

SCRIPT 1: LABELING NOT-OKAY TOUCHES

Child: Daddy, that boy pushed me off the slide!

Caregiver: Oh, that's a not-okay touch. I'm so glad you told me so I can help (gives child a hug).

Child: He's so mean.

Caregiver: It's okay for you to tell him that what he did is not okay. You got away from him and got help. It seems like he is still learning how to be nice. I think a good choice would be to stay away from him. How about we go play on the swing now?

Child: Yeah!

SCRIPT 2: INTRODUCING BUBBLE SPACE

Caregiver: Let's blow bubbles! Do you see how they're all different sizes?

Child: Yes, look how big that one is!

Caregiver: Whoa, it's so big! Oh, you popped it. Do you know we all have an invisible bubble around our body called our bubble space? (Make motion around your body.) You have a bubble space, too. (Make motion around the child's body.) This is your space, and you choose who's allowed to enter it. You can make it bigger when you want more space.

Child: I'm going to pop your bubble!

Caregiver: I'm your mom/dad, so our bubbles touch a lot. I love your cuddles and hugs, but for other people, we should ask permission if we want to go into their bubble. Like you might ask your friend if you can have a hug.

Child: My teacher does that.

Caregiver: That's great. Your teacher is respecting your bubble space. Just like these bubbles, your bubble might be big around a stranger and small around me. That's okay!

SCRIPT 3: TAKE A BREAK

Child: (Hits caregiver when they don't get a cookie.)

Caregiver (in a neutral voice): That hurts. You may not give not-okay touches.

Child: Then, give me a cookie!

Caregiver: I'm going to walk away because I do not want to be yelled at or hurt (walks to another room and closes the door).

Child: You're so mean! (Throws a fit. After a few minutes, the child quiets down and knocks on the door.)

Caregiver (opens the door): Thank you for quieting down.

Child: I'm sorry I hurt you (gives the caregiver a hug).

Caregiver: Thank you for saying you are sorry. When we are angry, it's good to take a break from the other person and do something relaxing. Let's take a deep breath together to practice (child and caregiver take deep breaths together).

Child: I feel better.

Caregiver: Good. It's never okay to hit. If I see you get angry, I'm going to say, "Take a break." That will be your clue that we will walk away from each other to calm down.

ACTIVITIES

Here are four activities you can weave into your interactions with your child to help teach and reinforce information about boundaries. You might pick one activity to do now, and do additional activities as your child gets older, or repeat activities as you'd like, making them more age appropriate as your child grows.

Shape Line Boundaries

Because the concept of boundaries is an abstract one, teaching your child about boundaries can be difficult to do in a concrete way.

Think about the saying "crossing the line" as it relates to a boundary. In coloring, we tell children to "stay in the lines." This activity uses the lines of a shape to help your child visualize body space boundaries with others.

MATERIALS
- Paper
- Crayons or markers in multiple colors

INSTRUCTIONS
1. Draw or make different shapes on a piece of paper.
2. Have your child color the shapes in different colors.
3. As they color, teach them that the lines of the shapes are their boundaries. Encourage them not to go past the boundary and to color in the lines.

NOTE: During this activity, make the connection between the shape boundaries and their body's boundaries. You could even touch your finger to the shape, then touch your finger to their arm to make the connection between boundaries.

DIY Bubble Space

After completing the previous activity, help your child create those boundaries around their body.

Once again, this exercise uses a concrete object to help your child visualize the personal space around their body and others' bodies. Remind them that we all have our own bubble space and each of us can decide who can come inside our bubble. Here, you'll use a circular object to represent bubble space. Use the ideas and discussion points in the note following to help reinforce the lesson.

MATERIALS
· Items that can make a circle (toilet paper, rope or string, Hula-Hoop)

INSTRUCTIONS
1. Create a circle with your material(s).
2. Climb into the circle or put it around your body and then your child's body.
3. Use the different props to show your child how they can make their bubble bigger for strangers and smaller for family members.
4. Talk with your child about bubbles and personal space.

NOTE: You can make different-size bubbles using painter's tape on the ground or chalk on a driveway or sidewalk. Invite your child to stand in the bubble they would choose for a friend, a stranger, a dog they don't know, or a family member. Take turns standing inside the bubble and talking about different scenarios. You might stand in the bubble and say, "I am angry," or "I need a hug," or "I am a stranger." Then, your child can decide whether it's a good idea to come into your space or stay outside the shape. Explain that if someone comes into their bubble after they tell them no, it's a not-okay touch.

Thumbs-Up or -Down Touches

As your child begins to understand personal space, they can make better sense of okay and not-okay touches.

There are plenty of touches that are clearly okay, like hugging a family member, or not-okay, such as hurting touches. These are the easiest touches to start with. Some other touches may or may not be okay, depending on the person and the situation. As your child progresses, initiate discussions on these more complex scenarios.

MATERIALS
- Paper
- Pencil or pen

INSTRUCTIONS
1. Write a list of okay and not-okay touches.
2. Show your child how to give a thumbs-up for okay touches and a thumbs-down for not-okay touches.
3. Read each example, and let your child respond with a thumbs-up or thumbs-down.
4. If they are unsure, coach or explain to them whether it's okay or not and why. Praise their efforts!

NOTE: Here are some ideas to get you started.

Okay Touches
- Hugging your parent
- High-fiving your teacher
- Handshake with a new friend
- Fist bump with the bus driver
- Cuddling with a grandparent

Not-Okay Touches
- Kissing your friend
- Hitting
- Touching private parts
- Kicking
- Hugging someone who doesn't want you to

Consider your family culture regarding kisses, hugs, etc. If someone in your child's life expects them to engage in touches that you or your child are not comfortable with, it's important to speak with that person. Explain what you are working on with your child and how you are coaching your child to respond to touches. This can help others understand your perspective and protect your child's boundaries, which (ideally) will help those moments go more smoothly.

Repeat It Back

Body boundaries are one way we respect each other. Another aspect of respect is listening to what others say, which is called "active listening." Active listening involves paying close attention to what the other person is saying so we can repeat it back, almost word for word.

This activity will introduce your child to the art of active listening, a valuable but challenging skill to master as they grow. Listening helps us respect other people's boundaries; after all, sometimes, we have to hear the boundary to be able to respect it.

MATERIALS
- Visual of listening ears, such as a picture of ears, Mr. or Mrs. Potato Head ears, etc. (optional)

INSTRUCTIONS
1. Say you are putting on your "listening ears." Ask your child to tell a short story.
2. When they finish, repeat their story. Ask whether you got it right.
3. Have your child take a turn, starting by having them put on their listening ears.
4. Tell your child a short story, then ask them to repeat it to you.
5. If they missed a major part, remind them of it and ask them to try again.

NOTE: Your story can be made up or real. You might start with a story about them to engage their interest. Include a few specific details for them to recall. Example: "Last week, we went to the park together and met a dog named Milo. He was very cute and let you pet him. But then it started to rain really hard, and we got wet running to our car." To increase the challenge, try a fictional story with more details and names. Praise them for the parts they remembered and for listening so carefully!

CHAPTER 3

Understanding Consent

AS YOUR CHILD begins to understand boundaries and okay versus not-okay touches, begin to introduce the concept of consent. Consent is granted when we explicitly tell someone they can enter our personal space or do an activity together. In this chapter, we explore how to help your child ask for okay touches from appropriate people, understand when they can give consent, and recognize when to get help from a trusted adult regarding consent.

WHY THIS, WHY NOW?

Important conversations about consent will continue throughout your child's development, but even at this young age, your child can benefit from learning the basics. These early teachings will give them the understanding they need to stop a behavior if someone asks them to or to keep their distance if someone does not want an okay touch.

Since consent goes both ways, they will learn that if they tell someone to stop a behavior that affects their personal space, that person should stop. If they tell someone they do not want a hug, that person should not hug them. By taking control of their body and boundaries, children can begin to assert themselves with others to stay safe and comfortable. These basic lessons will also set the groundwork for effective consent in later relationships, such as dating.

Vocabulary

We've talked about "**okay**" and "**not-okay**" touches—these terms describe consent in a way that's easy for a young child to grasp. When they're ready, the term "**consent**" takes their vocabulary to the next level. By using the word "consent" in discussions about boundaries, you help your child categorize when to use it and what to do if someone ignores their lack of consent.

CONVERSATION GUIDE

Once your child understands okay and not-okay touches and that we all have body boundaries, begin to introduce how to ask for okay touches and how to give consent for others to give them okay touches.

GETTING STARTED

Remind your child that everyone has an invisible bubble around them, which is their personal space. Some people's bubbles are bigger, and some are smaller. Use simple examples from their own life. For instance, they might have a friend who doesn't like hugs. That means their friend's bubble is bigger and that friend needs more space to feel comfortable. On the other hand, your child might feel okay with a smaller bubble because they like hugs. Similarly, if your child doesn't like giving Grandpa a hug, it's because their bubble is bigger when it comes to him. They should know it's okay to say no, even if Grandpa has a smaller bubble and likes hugs. When your child understands that everyone has their own bubble size, they'll know why it's important to ask before touching someone.

CONTINUING THE CONVERSATION

Sometimes, children need reminders to ask and then wait for an answer before giving okay touches. When this happens, ask for a "redo" and have them ask and wait for a yes before giving the okay touch. Do this when opportunities present themselves. You can also do pretend practice with your child, including how to say no to others when they request a not-okay touch. By practicing, your child will become more comfortable with saying no and not feel pressured into inter-actions that make them uncomfortable. Seeing you stand up for them can also build your child's confidence. If they tell Grandpa they don't want a hug and he persists, reassure them they don't have to give him a hug. If you wish, ask your child if they'd be comfortable with a handshake, high five, or fist bump. It's also okay for them to change their mind or ask for help if they aren't sure what to do.

SCRIPTS

Here are three scripts you can use as you discuss consent with your child. Script 1 is geared toward a three-year-old, script 2 to a four- or five-year-old, and script 3 to a six-year-old. Feel free to adapt these to meet your child where they are.

SCRIPT 1: BUBBLE PERMISSION

Caregiver: Remember how everyone has a body bubble? Before someone comes into your bubble, they should ask permission. Before you go into someone else's bubble, you should ask, too.

Child: Okay. Can we play now?

Caregiver: I'd love to play with you. (As you play with two cars or other toys):

"Hi, red car, can I give you a bump hello?"

"Yes, blue car, I'd like that." (Bump cars lightly together.)

Child: My car wants one, too!

Caregiver (lightly bumps their car): Thanks for telling me you wanted one, too. Now, my car knows it's okay to go into your car's bubble.

SCRIPT 2: HUGS—WITH PERMISSION

Caregiver: I love your hugs. I'm your caregiver, so you can give me hugs anytime, but we need to ask other people first if it's okay. If you make a new friend at the park and want to give them a hug when you say goodbye, you should say, "Can I give you a hug?"

Child: Hugs are nice.

Caregiver: Hugs are nice, but not everyone wants them. You should ask first, then wait for them to say yes (or no). Let's practice. Can I give you a hug?

Child: Yes!

Caregiver: Now, it's your turn to ask.

Child: Can I give you a hug? (Immediately hugs caregiver.)

Caregiver: Wait. Make sure the other person says yes first.

Child: Oops, I forgot. Can I give you a hug?

Caregiver: Yes (invites child to give a hug).

SCRIPT 3: NO HUGS ARE OKAY

Caregiver: I saw you didn't want to give Grandma a hug today.

Child: She squeezes so tight. I don't like it.

Caregiver: It's okay you didn't want a hug. You can tell her no if you don't want one. Next time, what could you do when she wants to hug you and you don't want one?

Child: I could tell her she squeezes too tight.

Caregiver: That's a great idea. She may not realize it feels so tight. You can decide if you want to try to hug with less squeeze or if you want to give her a different kind of touch, like a high five, or if you only want to wave goodbye.

Child: We can hug if she doesn't squeeze me so tight.

Caregiver: Okay, let's talk to her next time we see her and see how it feels. Then, you can decide what to do next.

Child: Okay, will you do it with me?

Caregiver: Of course. I'm always here to help you.

ACTIVITIES

Here are four activities you can weave into your interactions with your child to help teach and reinforce information about consent. You might pick one activity to do now, and do additional activities as your child gets older, or repeat activities as you'd like, making them more age appropriate as your child grows.

"Asking" Role Play

In this activity, you and your child will practice asking each other for okay touches and giving consent or declining the request.

This activity will help your child learn to listen for someone's answer before giving the requested touch. It will also increase their confidence in asking for permission.

INSTRUCTIONS

1. Explain to your child that you are going to ask each other for okay touches.
2. Ask for an okay touch, such as, "Can I have a high five?" If they say "yes," give them the okay touch. If they say "no," say something like, "I won't give you that touch because you said no. Thanks for telling me."
3. Take turns asking and responding. Offer praise!

NOTE: You may need to prompt them to say "yes" or "no" before jumping into the okay touch. Give them help if they need it. They may repeat what you said, and that's okay. You can also say "yes" sometimes and "no" sometimes to help coach them through each possibility.

Consent Song

By teaching your child they are special and that their body is one of a kind, you help them understand why others should respect them and their boundaries.

Songs are a great way for people to remember things—just look at "The Alphabet Song!" This singing activity is a fun and catchy way to practice saying positive words over and over. It also reinforces the concept of consent.

INSTRUCTIONS

To the tune of "Wheels on the Bus," sing and do the hand motions:

This is my body (point to chest).
It's all mine (give yourself a hug).
It's all mine (give yourself a hug).
It's all mine (give yourself a hug).
This is my body (point to chest).
It's all mine (give yourself a hug).
I am special (raise hands in the air).

To join my bubble (use a hand motion to indicate the bubble around your body),
You better ask (point finger out)!
You better ask (point finger out)!
You better ask (point finger out)!
To join my bubble (use a hand motion to indicate the bubble around your body),
You better ask (point finger out)!
I am special (raise hands in the air).

NOTE: Be prepared for your young child to take consent very seriously. They may begin correcting *you* for giving a hug without asking. That's okay! They need to try this out with safe people they love before they feel comfortable doing it with others. Use those experiences as practice opportunities, then begin to help them understand the gray areas of when consent is not necessary or is understood in the relationship. For example, once you start hugging a friend hello and goodbye every time you see them, you may not need to ask before giving them a hug.

Red, Yellow, Green Light

This activity explores when it's okay to give consent for certain touches and with certain people. It also shows children that they may not always know the right answer—and that's okay.

The "yellow" in this game teaches your child they can ask a trusted grown-up when they aren't sure of what to do. This activity also reinforces okay and not-okay touches and that it's okay to set boundaries for not-okay touches. Do this activity seated together, or set paper with red, yellow, and green circles on the floor, and invite your child to hop on the correct color for each situation.

MATERIALS
· Paper
· Red, yellow, and green crayons or markers

INSTRUCTIONS
1. Draw or make a traffic light with red, yellow, and green circles.
2. Make a list of situations (see note following).
3. Explain that red means stop/say no; green means go/give consent; and yellow means slow down/ask a safe grown-up first.
4. For each situation you read, invite your child to point to or say the color. Give lots of praise!

NOTE: Here are some ideas to get you started. Feel free to come up with your own, using familiar people and situations. Reinforce that you're there to help if your child is unsure.

Red Examples

- Someone touching your private parts
- Someone trying to push you
- A stranger trying to hug you
- Any time you feel uncomfortable

Yellow Examples

- New friend wants to hug
- Parent's friend asking to tickle you
- New teacher inviting you to sit on their lap
- Stranger trying to give you a fist bump when a caregiver is present

Green Examples

- Hugs from family and friends
- High fives from teachers
- Handshake to a parent's friend
- Pat on the back from a coach

Changing Your Mind Story

This story activity is meant to help your child understand they can change their mind at any time regarding consent. It is imperative that they know other people need to respect their "no" or "stop" right away at any time in an interaction. It also demonstrates that we can keep our boundaries even if someone else does not like it or disagrees (a great lesson for us all!).

Teaching your child that they are not responsible for other people's happiness will help empower them to set boundaries that feel right to them.

MATERIALS

The following story:

Jane lives with her mom and her little brother. Her Aunt Shay comes to help every Saturday. Jane loves reading books and singing songs with Aunt Shay. One day, Aunt Shay wanted to play Tickle Monster. Jane thought it sounded fun and told Aunt Shay she would like to play Tickle Monster and get tickles. After a couple of seconds, Jane didn't like it anymore. Her belly hurt from the tickles. She told Aunt Shay to stop because it hurt. Aunt Shay stopped and frowned and said she wanted to keep playing. She looked sad. Jane didn't know what to do. She didn't want to play Tickle Monster, but she also didn't want to make Aunt Shay sad.

INSTRUCTIONS

1. Read the story with your child.
2. Discuss the following questions together:
    *   What should Jane do next?
    *   Why is Aunt Shay sad?
    *   What should Aunt Shay do next?
    *   Is it okay to change your mind about your body and touches?

NOTE: As you explore these questions together, here are some helpful discussion points:

*   It's okay to suggest another game or ask for a break.
*   Aunt Shay thinks the Tickle Monster game is fun, but Jane does not. They don't agree.
*   Aunt Shay should respect Jane's decision and find a different game to play with Jane.
*   We get to decide who and how someone touches our body.
*   It's okay to be done or change our mind.

CHAPTER 4

Defining Private Parts

PRIVATE PARTS CAN be a sensitive subject for many parents. If you haven't already done so, take time to teach your child the proper names of private parts. With children, we can call them the "doctor's names" of private parts to help them understand there are proper and slang words for these parts. Explaining what "private" means is also helpful as you introduce these words by saying that private is when you want to keep something to yourself, like those parts of your body that are only for you.

WHY THIS, WHY NOW?

If you introduce these words for private parts just like you teach them arm, leg, and foot, you'll make your child comfortable using proper language. If your child uses this language, they'll be clear to anyone they are speaking to. Everyone knows the names of these parts, even if they don't use the words in their everyday language. This will help your child be clearly understood if a safety problem arises or if they are trying to set boundaries with others regarding their body and personal space.

Vocabulary

The anatomically correct names for private parts include "**buttocks/butt**" for everyone; "**vagina**," "**vulva**," and "**breasts**" for females, and "**penis**" and "**testicles**" for males. When your child is ready, add additional words to this category (such as "**labia**," "**clitoris**," "**scrotum**") as questions or issues come up.

CONVERSATION GUIDE

Talking about private parts with your child can be awkward, but it's important. Don't worry if it makes you uncomfortable. The more you have these conversations and use the proper names for private body parts, the more comfortable you and your child will become.

GETTING STARTED

Labeling body parts is a great way to start the conversation about private parts. For example, when toilet training, tell a male to point his penis down or direct a female to wipe her vagina. By using the proper names, your child will learn them without a separate conversation or activity. Reiterating these terms in everyday life is the best way to build comfort and ease around these concepts.

Once they understand the names of each private part, you can also explain to your child why they are called private parts. These parts are private—only for them to see and touch—and no one else should see or touch them. That is why we wear underwear and bathing suits. Of course, there are exceptions to every rule. Remind them that, sometimes, caregivers and doctors need to see or touch their private parts, such as when there is something wrong or if they have a question. If you are still helping with toileting and bathing, explain this is another exception because you're still teaching them how to clean their private parts and keeping them safe while they bathe.

CONTINUING THE CONVERSATION

As your child gets older and gains autonomy in toileting and bathing, there are fewer opportunities to label private parts in real-life settings. You may need to initiate conversations or take advantage of various opportunities as they arise. For example, if a friend at school uses a slang word, talk about slang words versus the doctor's names of private parts. By showing (or faking!) your comfort with these topics, your child will come to you with questions.

SCRIPTS

Here are three scripts you can use to further teach your child the proper names of private parts. Script 1 is geared toward a three-year-old, script 2 to a four- or five-year-old, and script 3 to a six-year-old. Feel free to adapt these to meet your child where they are.

SCRIPT 1: POTTY TRAINING AND PRIVATE PARTS

Caregiver (to child getting dressed): Your underwear covers your private parts. The part you pee out of is called your vagina/penis. The part you poop out of is called your butt.

Child: Do you have a butt?

Caregiver: Everyone has a butt, but males and females have different parts that they pee out of. Males have a penis, and females have a vagina. Can you say them with me?

Child and caregiver together: Vagina and penis.

SCRIPT 2: POTTY TRAINING: PRIVATE PARTS 2

Child: I need to go potty.

Caregiver: Great job telling me. Let's go.

Child: (Gets on the toilet.)

Caregiver: Remember to wipe your vagina and butt.

Child: I will!

Caregiver: Nice job going potty.

Child: My butt hurts.

Caregiver: Sometimes, when we poop, our butt hurts. Do you need help?

Child: No, it's better now. Let's go back to the party.

SCRIPT 3: MALE PRIVATE PARTS

Child: Today, Johnny grabbed his pants and said his pee-wee hurts. What's a pee-wee?

Caregiver: Some people call their penis a pee-wee, but we use the doctor's name and call that part your penis.

Child: Pee-wee is funny!

Caregiver: Pee-wee sounds funny to you, but not everyone knows what that means. If you say penis, everyone will understand what you mean. That's important if you need help.

ACTIVITIES

Here are four activities you can weave into your interactions with your child to help teach and reinforce information about the proper names of private parts and safety. You might pick one activity to do now, and do additional activities as your child gets older, or repeat activities as you'd like, making them more age appropriate as your child grows.

Identifying Body Parts

This activity will teach your child which body parts are private and the doctor's names for each body part.

Start with a drawing of a same-sex child as your child, then discuss or repeat the activity with the other gender.

MATERIALS
- Paper
- Crayons or markers

INSTRUCTIONS
1. Draw a picture of a child with a swimsuit on.
2. Tell your child you are going to name the body parts with them.
3. Ask them to circle the following body parts: head, neck, chest, stomach, arms, hands, penis/vagina, butt, legs, and feet.
4. Praise them when they are correct and help them if needed.

NOTE: Tell your child that we wear a swimsuit because it covers our private parts, which are not for others to see.

Private Parts Circle of Trust

This activity will help you and your child discuss the small circle of safe grown-ups they can trust and go to if they need help with their private parts or touches others may give them.

The main adults to consider safe are caregivers and the doctor (with a caregiver present). This might include parents, grandparents, aunts or uncles, teachers, or babysitters you know very well. You can also have your child draw a picture of the doctor, and reiterate that doctors can help with private parts just like they help with other body parts.

MATERIALS
- Paper
- Crayons or markers

INSTRUCTIONS
1. Ask your child to draw a picture of a safe grown-up in their life who can help them if something is wrong, including with their private parts.
2. Explain that no one else should see or touch their private parts, including other children.

NOTE: Your child may be curious or uncomfortable about the idea of someone seeing or touching their private parts, so be open to their questions and remind them these trusted people are there for them if they need help with their privates or anything else. Remind them to tell you if someone touches them in a way that feels uncomfortable or "yucky."

Stop, Go, Tell

Saying no can be hard. In this activity, your child will practice saying no or telling someone to stop if they are about to touch your child in an unwanted way.

Repeat this easy role-playing exercise so it will become automatic and easy for your child to do in the moment. After they tell the person to **stop** (or say no), they should try to get away from them (**go**) and then find a grown-up to **tell**. By repeating "stop, go, tell," you're helping your child remember the steps. When discussing who to tell, refer back to the safe grown-ups in their life.

INSTRUCTIONS

1. Explain that you are going to play "Stop, Go, Tell."
2. Have your child practice yelling "stop" and running across the room.
3. Tell your child you're going to pretend to be a child giving them a not-okay touch and you want them to stop, go, and tell.
4. Raise your hand and say, "I'm pretending to hit you. What should you do?" Coach them to say "stop" or "no" and run.
5. Praise your child for their good work. Tell them you are their safe grown-up and they can tell you what happened.

NOTE: If your child has a hard time understanding, you might model "Stop, Go, Tell" for them first and then give them a turn. Coach your child to tell you "what happened," and praise them for telling you when they felt unsafe. If your child has a history of trauma, you might verbally describe the not-okay touch instead of making a hitting motion.

You Are Special, You Are Safe

This activity will help build your child's confidence in who they are and what they should do to be safe.

When a child has confidence, they are more likely to use "Stop, Go, Tell" strategies in difficult situations. Also show them they already do many things to be safe, and praise them for being brave and remembering their safety and the safety of others.

MATERIALS
- Paper
- Pencil or pen

INSTRUCTIONS
1. Draw an outline of your child's hands on paper.
2. Ask them to share some good things about themselves.
3. As they share, write each quality in a left finger on the paper as you say it out loud.
4. Ask them to share things they do to be safe.
5. As they share, write each item in a right finger as you say it out loud.

NOTE: If they name more than five things in either category, write them on the corresponding palm. Conversely, if they need help thinking of good things, ask, "What makes you a good friend?" "What are you good at?" or "What do you like about yourself?" As you write the responses, reiterate that you think it is a great thing about them, too. If they need help thinking of things they do to be safe, give them prompts like "What do you do in the car to be safe?" (Wear a seatbelt.) Or "What do you do before you cross a street?" (Look both ways or hold a grown-up's hand.)

CHAPTER 5

Talking About Your Needs

WE ALL HAVE different preferences regarding how we are touched by others. Some people may have large bubbles for everyone; others may have smaller bubbles for everyone. When we meet someone, we don't automatically know their preferences. Likewise, no one knows our preferences unless we tell them. While we can't read each other's minds, we can often use body language for clues. Otherwise, it's best to be direct and speak up. These nuances are all part of life. This chapter will help you build the foundation early for your child.

WHY THIS, WHY NOW?

By teaching your child at a young age that everyone has different preferences and that, sometimes, we need to tell people our preferences directly, your child can practice this skill throughout childhood and master it by the time they are a teenager. If they become comfortable setting boundaries, they'll be able to speak up when someone tries to push those boundaries. Just like the other topics in this book, we can introduce this to children as soon as they learn to say no and yes. Think about this: When they begin to express their preferences about what foods to eat or what toys to play with, they can begin to tell you how they prefer to be touched.

Vocabulary

Preferences are used to help communicate how your child prefers to be touched by others. Introducing preferences with your child's strong likes will help them understand what you mean. For example, you might name their favorite food or movie as their preference for what to eat or watch. Then, you can describe preferences for touches. Maybe your child prefers to give you hugs and their friends high fives. There are a lot of different types of touches, and we may prefer some over the others. Those are our preferences.

CONVERSATION GUIDE

Introduce this topic organically in everyday life, then follow up with more pointed conversations as needed. As you give your child the opportunity to communicate their preferences with you and others, and praise them when they do so, they will gain confidence to speak up when someone pushes back on their boundaries.

GETTING STARTED

Look for discussion opportunities in your daily life. For example, when you are tickling your child and they tell you to stop, stop and say, "I'm going to stop because I heard you say 'stop,' and we should listen when someone tells us they don't want us to touch them." Another great way for your child to learn boundaries is by watching you model boundaries. If they see you communicating your preferences with them and other people in your life, they will be more comfortable doing it. For example, if your child is hanging on you while you are eating dinner, you might say, "Please don't hang on me while I'm eating. I don't want to spill my food and need some space." When they climb off you, praise them for respecting your boundaries.

CONTINUING THE CONVERSATION

As your child gets older and spends more time with their peers, coach them through those moments when peers push boundaries or make them uncomfortable. This coaching might happen in the moment if, for example, you are present during a playdate. Sometimes, the coaching happens after the incident has occurred, such as when they get home from school. Role-playing is a great way to reinforce skills like this so your child can practice what they could say differently next time. If they're unsure what to say, let them pretend they are the peer and you're your child so you can model what to say and they can express how the peer might respond.

SCRIPTS

Here are three scripts you can use to discuss personal preferences with your child. Script 1 is geared toward a three-year-old, script 2 to a four- or five-year-old, and script 3 to a six-year-old. Feel free to adapt these to meet your child where they are.

SCRIPT 1: INTRODUCING GIVING AN ALTERNATIVE TOUCH

Child: Mommy! Huggie! (Tries to give fifth hug in 10 minutes.)

Caregiver (doing laundry): Actually, hon, how about a high five instead?

Child: Mommy! Huggie!

Caregiver: I'm happy to give you a high five right now, but I need a break from hugs while I finish the laundry.

Child: Fine (walks away).

Caregiver (finishes the laundry and finds the child in their room): Hon, I'm sorry your feelings are hurt. Sometimes, I need to do tasks for our family. I finished the laundry. Do you still want a hug?

Child: No, meanie.

Caregiver: Okay. Well, when you're ready, I can give you a hug.

SCRIPT 2: HOW TO SAY "NO" TO A TOUCH

Caregiver: You know we all have different ways we like to be touched. Other people don't know what we like unless we tell them. Do you like when I give you hugs?

Child: Yes, I love your hugs. And Grammy's hugs, too.

Caregiver: What if someone you don't remember tried to hug you, like one of my old friends?

Child: Ew, no. I don't want to hug them.

Caregiver: That's okay. I might give them a hug because they're my friend from a long time ago. Since you don't know them, it's okay for you not to give them a hug. What should you do if they put their hands out for a hug?

Child: I don't know.

Caregiver: You can just say, "No, thank you. I don't want a hug."

Child: Will they cry?

Caregiver: Maybe, but that's okay. They can get a hug from someone else. It doesn't need to be you.

Child: Good. I don't know if I can say that, though.

Caregiver: That's okay, I'll help you!

SCRIPT 3: WHEN SOMEONE DOESN'T LISTEN TO "NO"

Caregiver: Your friend Tony is coming over today.

Child: Yay! I'm going to build a tower with him.

Caregiver: Oh, that sounds fun.

Child (frowns, thinking): Sometimes, Tony likes to wrestle. I don't want to do that.

Caregiver: Hmm. It sounds like Tony likes to wrestle, and you don't. What do you think you can tell him if he asks to play wrestle?

Child: No?

Caregiver: That's right! You can tell him, "No, I don't want to do that." Maybe you can give him an idea of something else to play, like tossing a ball.

Child: I can try. Sometimes, Tony doesn't listen, and he just wrestles me anyway.

Caregiver: Well, you can say your "no" a little louder and come get me if you need help. It's okay to keep telling him you don't want to wrestle.

Child: Thanks, Mom. Maybe you can stay in the kitchen so you can hear me.

Caregiver (nodding): I'll do that.

ACTIVITIES

Here are four activities you can weave into your interactions with your child to help teach and reinforce information about setting direct and firm boundaries. You might pick one activity to do now, and do additional activities as your child gets older, or repeat activities as you'd like, making them more age appropriate as your child grows.

The Right Touch Art

Helping your child brainstorm how they prefer to be touched in different situations will solidify when they might feel comfortable giving a touch and when they might want to say no to a touch.

In addition to exploring preferred touches, this activity also explores alternative touches your child can use if someone is trying to give them a non-preferred touch.

MATERIALS
· Paper
· Crayons or markers

INSTRUCTIONS
1. Remind your child we all have touches we prefer from different people. Ask them to draw a picture of them doing their favorite touch with you.
2. When they're done, talk about their picture and what you like about it.
3. Repeat this activity, first having the child draw themself with a friend, then with a teacher.

NOTE: If your child draws a picture of a touch the other person might not prefer or enjoy, discuss the other person's perspective. For example, if they draw a picture of them kissing a friend, explain that most children do not kiss children outside their family. You can suggest your child draw a picture of a high five instead. Take the conversation further, discussing how they might feel if that person said no to their preferred touch and how the other person might feel if your child gave that touch anyway.

Saying "No" Role Play

It can be uncomfortable saying no to someone, but the more you practice saying no, the easier it gets.

This activity will help your child get used to saying no whenever needed.

INSTRUCTIONS

1. Tell your child you will take turns asking for touches and saying no.
2. As you practice, express different responses of feelings to their "no," such as acting indifferent, sad, mad, or scared.
3. Give praise and reassurance that it's okay to keep their boundary even if the other person seems upset. They don't need to change their "no."

NOTE: You can also model for your child how to say no and offer an alternative okay touch you feel more comfortable giving; for example, "I don't want a handshake, but I'll give you a fist bump."

Others' Feelings Story

This story is meant to help your child understand they don't have to compromise their comfort zone to make someone else happy.

Sometimes, people get upset about our boundaries, but that's okay.

MATERIALS
The following story:

Joe is feeling grumpy today, and he has to go to his cousin's birthday party. When he gets there, he stands behind his parents as everyone says hello. He doesn't feel like giving hugs and kisses. His grandma and grandpa wave and say hi. He waves back and tries to sneak past into the playroom.

His uncle catches him and asks, "Where's my hug?"

Joe says, "I don't want any hugs today."

Uncle Pat says, "That makes me sad. It's not fair because I do want hugs today. Come on, give me a hug." Joe's uncle frowns, pretends to cry, and holds out his arms.

INSTRUCTIONS
1. Read the story to your child.
2. Ask them the following questions and discuss their answers.
   - What should Joe do?
   - Why is Uncle Pat upset?
   - What should Uncle Pat do?
   - What should Joe do if Uncle Pat hugs him without permission?

NOTE: As you explore these questions together, here are some helpful discussion points:

- It's okay to say "no" and try to get away from a person if you need to.
- If you wish, offer an alternate touch, such as a high five.
- People should respect one another's boundaries.
- If someone ignores your boundary, it's okay to say "stop" and tell a grown-up.

Every person has different expectations for children for greetings and goodbyes. It can be helpful to talk with family members about what you are teaching your child about body safety. This way, they can ask about touches rather than expecting them and be more prepared to respect a decline to their request.

"Someone Won't Stop" Role Play

Sometimes, people don't listen when your child tells them "no." It's important to practice through role-playing so your child feels prepared when this happens.

This role-playing activity will help your child begin to learn how to stick to their no and create boundaries, even with a grown-up.

INSTRUCTIONS

Take turns asking for touches, then keep pushing for the touch while the other person practices saying no and getting away from the person. Here's one example:

> *"Can I tickle you?"*
> *"No."*
> *"Please, it's so much fun! Let's tickle."*
> *"No, I don't like tickling."*
> *"Come on, I'm going to tickle you."*
> *"No!" (Runs away and tells a grown-up.)*

NOTE: Practice this activity using different scenarios, like pushing or hugging.

If your child doesn't understand what to do, coach them by modeling this exchange, either alone or with another family member. Offer lots of praise for your child's efforts! Ask them how it feels when someone doesn't listen to them and how it feels to stick up for their boundaries.

CHAPTER 6

Being Direct About Body Autonomy

SOMETIMES, PEOPLE DON'T respond well when we express a boundary. They might become upset and continue to push our boundary to get what they want, like Uncle Pat (see chapter 5). We often have to be direct to avoid misinterpretation. For this reason, it's important for children to learn assertiveness to keep them safe. If they are passive with others, at the very least, they're likely to get pushed over and not get their needs met.

WHY THIS, WHY NOW?

We can start to prepare our children at a young age for what to do when someone doesn't listen to their preferences. This can be challenging because, historically, children have been taught to be passive with adults. Passivity has been equated with respect; however, we can teach our children to be assertive and respectful at the same time. This shift in perspective can be difficult to understand, particularly for older generations, which is why it's helpful to have similar conversations with the adults in your child's life.

Vocabulary

When your child is old enough, it's time to define what bribes and threats are so they can begin to understand the concept of coercion. Coercion involves using inappropriate methods to try to get someone to do what you want. This coercion might be in the form of a bribe—that is, when someone offers a reward for giving them what they want. For example, "I'll give you a new toy if you give me a hug." It could also be in the form of a threat, such as when someone says they will do something the child doesn't want if the child does not do what they want. For example, "If you don't give me a hug, I'm going to take all your toys home with me."

CONVERSATION GUIDE

Young children tend to think in black and white—it's right or wrong; it's okay or not okay; you say no, and people listen. However, as adults, we recognize there's a lot of "gray" in the world. We want our children to learn to understand and know how to respond to those less concrete situations, such as when someone doesn't respect their expressed boundaries.

GETTING STARTED

There are several ways to start this conversation. You can point out a time when they pushed a boundary, such as begging for a toy at the store after you said no or climbing on the couch after being told to get down. Explain that, sometimes, other children and adults do the same. Modeling for your child how you stick to your boundaries with them is another great way for them to learn. You can also have more curated conversations as situations arise, like, "Did you see how that child kept pushing his brother after he said 'stop'?" to help solidify your child's learning.

Also, explain they can say no and then get away from the person as a way to avoid someone pushing their boundary. Tell your child to come to you about these situations so you can address them with the child and the person pushing their boundary if needed.

CONTINUING THE CONVERSATION

As your child gets older, deepen the conversation about how to respond to someone pushing their boundaries. Now, they can also have conversations with the people pushing their boundary after it has occurred or set expectations before-hand. As your child matures, also teach them about coercion and how people might use bribes or threats to get what they want. By defining those terms and discussing examples, you'll help your child recognize when someone is using those means. Reinforce that if someone uses bribes or threats, your child should say no or stop, get away from that person, and get help from a grown-up (see Stop, Go, Tell, page 62).

SCRIPTS

Here are three scripts you can use as you teach your child how to be direct. Script 1 is geared toward a three-year-old, script 2 to a four- or five-year-old, and script 3 to a six-year-old. Feel free to adapt these to meet your child where they are.

SCRIPT 1: GETTING AWAY WHEN SOMEONE DOESN'T STOP

Caregiver: Sometimes, people don't listen when we say no or stop. Let's say someone gave you a hug after you said you didn't want one.

Child: That's mean.

Caregiver: You're right. When someone says no to a touch, we're supposed to listen and respect them by not giving the touch. If someone doesn't listen to you when you say no and hug you anyway, what do you think you should do?

Child: Run away!

Caregiver: Yes, you can get away from them and find a grown-up who can help, like me or your teacher. What if they don't let you leave and keep holding you in the hug?

Child: I'll kick them.

Caregiver: You should always try to use your words first, but if that doesn't work, it's okay to yell at them loudly or push them to try to get away. When you get away, quickly find a grown-up and tell them what happened.

SCRIPT 2: HOW A SAFE GROWN-UP CAN HELP

Caregiver: I noticed that [name of person in child's life] always tries to give you hugs [or other touches] when they see you in the hallway, and you don't seem to like it.

Child: I told them I don't want hugs, but they don't listen to me. I guess the hugs aren't so bad.

Caregiver: It's up to you if you want a hug. If you don't want hugs, they should listen to you. Should we tell them together?

Child: As long as you are there. They won't listen to me.

Caregiver: Oh, yes. We will do it together. Let's practice what we're going to say. How about something like this? "[Name of person], I've noticed that [child's name] does not want hugs from you, but you hug them anyway. It is very important to [child's name] and me that you listen and respect their boundaries. Please don't give them hugs anymore. They'd prefer a wave."

Child: Oooh, that's a good idea. Thanks!

Caregiver: Of course, we will get this done together. You shouldn't have to get a hug if you don't want one.

SCRIPT 3: COERCION, BRIBES, AND THREATS

Caregiver: Let's talk about coercion. That's a big word, but it just means someone is trying to get you to do something you don't want to do. We've talked about that before, like when someone wants a hug but you don't want one. Remember?

Child: Yeah, I remember! Uncle Pat did that!

Caregiver: Yes, well, sometimes, people use bribes or threats to get what they want. A bribe is when someone says they will give you what you want if you do what they want, like, "I'll give you a piece of candy if you give me a hug."

Child: Oh, candy!

Caregiver: It's important to remember what's best for your body, though. If you actually want to give that person a hug, it's okay. If you are only giving them a hug to get the candy, that's not okay, and you will end up feeling yucky afterward.

Child: I guess—and candy isn't healthy.

Caregiver: Sometimes, people also use threats to get what they want. A threat is when they say something bad will happen if you don't give them what they want, like, "If you don't give me a hug, then I won't play with you."

Child: That's not nice!

Caregiver: No, it's not. And most people will not actually do the bad thing anyway, so it's best to just say no and tell a grown-up what happened.

Child: Like you! I'll come tell you!

Caregiver: Yes, that's a wonderful idea. If you're at school, you can tell your teacher, then tell me when you get home.

Child: Okay! Can we play the game now?

Caregiver: Yes, I love talking and playing with you.

ACTIVITIES

Here are four activities you can weave into your interactions with your child to help teach and reinforce saying no to not-okay touches. You might pick one activity to do now, and do additional activities as your child gets older, or repeat activities as you'd like, making them more age appropriate as your child grows.

"Why Not?" Role Play

This role-play activity will teach your child how to stay firm in saying no when someone is pushing them to give in.

By modeling how to say no, you'll equip your child with words and body language they can use when they need to say no to someone.

INSTRUCTIONS

1. Tell your child to ask for a hug.
2. In response, say no, then tell your child to ask "Why not?" to whatever you say.
3. Hold firm to your no as they continue to ask, "Why not?" After three "Why not?" questions, walk away from your child.
4. Switch roles and invite them to be the person saying no.

NOTE: You can use different types of responses or just say no. Other responses might include "I'm not in the mood" or "I don't want a hug. Please stop." Model how to say no with body language by putting up a hand, shaking your head, crossing your arms, or frowning.

No! and Stop!

It can be uncomfortable to go from assertive to aggressive. Practicing together will help your child gain confidence in getting louder and more aggressive if the need arises.

We want our children to be respectfully assertive. However, in rare instances, it can become necessary to respond more aggressively.

INSTRUCTIONS

1. Tell your child you are going to take turns yelling "NO!" and "STOP!" Do this for three to five rounds.
2. Reinforce that these yelling words are only used in unsafe situations, not when a grown-up is telling them to do a chore or homework. Explain that if they need to use this voice, they should also get away from the person right away and get help from a safe grown-up.

NOTE: Remind your child that we always want to start with respectfully telling someone no or to stop. If that doesn't work and they continue to try to do what we don't want them to do, then it's okay to be louder and more aggressive. It's okay if you or your child laugh through this activity. It can feel silly to do this with each other. Laughter helps your child understand this is just an activity, not something they will ever need to say to you in a serious way.

When Is No Okay?

We teach our children to listen to adults and follow directions so it can be difficult for young children to understand that there are times when it's okay to say no to adults.

Saying no isn't an option when it comes to getting ready in the morning or following directions at school. This activity helps them understand appropriate times to say no.

MATERIALS
- Paper
- Light-colored crayons or markers
- Dark marker for writing

INSTRUCTIONS
1. Draw large bubble letters spelling "NO."
2. Invite your child to color the bubble letters using a light color. Explain that you will be writing on top of their drawing.
3. Ask your child, "Is it okay to say no when . . ." questions (see note following).
4. Use a marker to write okay/acceptable reasons inside the bubble letters and unacceptable reasons outside the letters.

NOTE: Here are some ideas to get you started.

Acceptable Reasons to Say No
- Someone asking for a hug
- Someone offering you food
- Someone asking to tickle you
- Someone asking for something that belongs to you

Unacceptable Reasons to Say No
· Teacher asks you to put away the toys
· Daddy asks you to brush your teeth
· Babysitter asks you to go to bed
· Friend asks you to stop touching them

Also, talk about the differences between saying no to grown-ups versus saying no to other children, such as if a teacher asks them to give them the toy they're playing with as opposed to a child asking.

"Broken Record No" Role Play

This role-playing activity will reiterate that it's okay to just keep saying no if needed.

Depending on the child's comprehension level, include different ways of asking or examples of bribes and threats as the other person continues to say no.

INSTRUCTIONS

1. Tell your child they are going to practice saying no.
2. Ask them for a touch. They should reply no.
3. Ask with more urgency ("C'mon, please?") or bribes ("If you give me a hug, I'll give you $200.") or threats ("If you don't give me a hug, I'll tell your teacher you hit me.").
4. Prompt them to keep saying no.
5. Take turns, switching roles.

NOTE: Afterward, discuss bribes and threats. Ask your child if it was tempting to change their mind and why they shouldn't change their mind (particularly for not-okay touches). Praise them for staying firm. Be sure to do this activity another time, using something like touching or looking at private parts, because that's a touch we should always say no to, no matter what.

CHAPTER 7

Identifying Safe Grown-Ups

AS YOUR CHILD learns about safety, it's important that they know which adults they can go to when they need help with boundary issues. By identifying safe grown-ups, children will know who they can go to when they feel uncomfortable or when someone gives a not-okay touch or ignores their "stop" or "no." Ideally, they will have at least one safe adult in each setting where they spend a significant amount of time. For example, at home, their safe adult can be their caregivers; at daycare or school, their safe adult can be their teachers.

WHY THIS, WHY NOW?

Babies learn very quickly that there are people who take care of them and keep them safe. This knowledge builds their sense of safety in the world. They learn this when someone responds to their crying and reliably meets their needs, even when caregivers don't get it right on the first try. As babies grow into toddlers, they continue to learn who keeps them safe. Maybe Mom catches them when they are about to fall or Dad buckles them into their car seat, but now they also know their favorite aunt takes good care of them when they're sick and their teacher helps keep them safe from not-okay touches. As their world expands, children discover other trusted caregivers and adult family members are also available to help them keep their body safe and healthy.

Vocabulary

Children need clear and direct language to guide them. By describing caregivers as **"safe grown-ups"** or **"safe adults,"** you give your child clear guidance on who they should go to when they feel unsafe.

CONVERSATION GUIDE

By age three, your child is likely calling the adults in their life by name. This developmental milestone can signify a good opportunity to talk about who the safe adults in their life are.

GETTING STARTED

Add real-life examples of how their safe grown-ups have helped them in various situations. If Grandma helped them when they tripped and fell, remind them that Grandma is a safe grown-up because she helps. By directly linking the person to the term "safe grown-up," your child can easily identify who to go to if they need help. No matter who their safe grown-ups are, reinforce to your child that they should also tell you about any unsafe situations. This way, you can make sure the situation was addressed to your satisfaction. Sometimes, adults fail to act and may not even advise you that an incident occurred. If your child tells you what happened and so does the safe adult, it provides assurance on two levels—that your child knows to communicate with you and that they are in good hands in that person's care.

CONTINUING THE CONVERSATION

Most of the safe adults in your child's life are going to be familiar faces in each of their settings. However, what does a child do when there is no familiar face around? Have a discussion with your child about how to identify strangers who are more likely to be safe. On the rare occasion your child has no one they know present, having a plan will lessen their anxiety. Make a plan together for what they will do by teaching them to find the "helpers" in public places. These helpers can be police officers, firefighters, park rangers, and doctors. Sometimes, those people may not be around, in which case the next set of helpers might be the people who work there, such as other teachers at a school or retail workers in a store. Teach your child to look for someone wearing a name tag and explain how to approach that person when they need help. You can also help them identify other mothers or fathers who might help if they get lost at the playground or supermarket or somewhere with no other helpers around.

SCRIPTS

Here are three scripts you can use to discuss safe grown-ups. Script 1 is geared toward a three-year-old, script 2 to a four- or five-year-old, and script 3 to a six-year-old. Feel free to adapt these to meet your child where they are.

SCRIPT 1: IDENTIFYING SAFE GROWN-UPS

Child: I love Pappy.

Caregiver: You love Pappy, and Pappy is a safe grown-up. He will help you if you need it.

Child: He gave me a bandage and an ice pop when I fell.

Caregiver: That's right! Pappy can help you be safe. If you have a problem and Pappy is around, you can tell him about it, okay?

Child: Okay.

Caregiver: And whatever you tell Pappy, tell me, too. I want to do everything I can to keep you safe.

Child: I can tell you, too.

Caregiver: That's great because, sometimes, even safe grown-ups don't know what to do, and we need to keep telling other grown-ups until someone can help.

Child: Oh. Can I draw a picture for Pappy?

Caregiver: Yes! Let's go to the table.

SCRIPT 2: TELLING VERSUS TATTLING

Caregiver: Hi, hon. Remember we were talking about safe grown-ups? Who are some of your safe grown-ups?

Child: Mama, Dada, Papa, Nana, Ms. Lori, and the police.

Caregiver: That's wonderful! What are some things you might tell a safe grown-up?

Child: If someone hits me.

Caregiver: Yes, if someone gives you or tries to give you any not-okay touches, like hurting touches or touching privates, you definitely should tell a safe grown-up. What if someone takes your toy? Should you tell on them?

Child: Yeah, that's mean, too.

Caregiver: Well, use your words first and ask them to give the toy back to you. If they won't give it back and you feel like hitting them or they hit you, then you can tell a grown-up. Sometimes, children don't get along and grown-ups don't need to hear about every single problem. Can you think of a time when another kid did something you didn't like?

Child: Remember when Megan called me a meanie and stuck her tongue out at me? I didn't like that.

Caregiver: Ooh, that's a good example. It wasn't nice, but you didn't need to tell a grown-up right away about that. Instead, you just told me about it when you got home from school so we could talk about your feelings and come up with a plan.

SCRIPT 3: FINDING SAFE GROWN-UPS IN PUBLIC

Caregiver: Hey, bud. What do you think you should do if we are at the park and you can't find me?

Child: I would cry!

Caregiver: If that ever happens, you might cry, but you can be brave, too. Who do you think could help you if that happens?

Child: Hmm, police?

Caregiver: That's true. If you see a police officer or park ranger, they could definitely help you. They aren't always at the park, though, so who else could help you?

Child: I don't know. I can't talk to strangers.

Caregiver: Well, that might be a time when only strangers are around you. You can find a mommy/daddy who is playing with their children and ask for help finding me.

Child: Would you help if a kid asked you?

Caregiver: Of course I would! Do you remember what my real name is?

Child: Ryan!

Caregiver: That's right. You could tell the other mommy/daddy you need help finding your daddy named Ryan. They will help you find me.

Child: I don't want that to happen.

Caregiver: Me neither, bud. That's why I always keep an eye on you, and we stay together when we are out. That way, we can be safe.

ACTIVITIES

Here are four activities you can weave into your interactions with your child to help teach and reinforce information about safe grown-ups. You might pick one activity to do now, and do additional activities as your child gets older, or repeat activities as you'd like, making them more age appropriate as your child grows.

Identifying Safe Grown-Ups

In this activity, you'll engage in direct conversations with your child about who their safe grown-ups are.

As your child learns which grown-ups they can turn to for help, continue to reinforce the idea throughout their daily life.

INSTRUCTIONS

1. Tell your child you are going to name and/or show pictures of grown-ups, and they will indicate whether each person is a safe grown-up or not. Include caregivers, adult family members or friends, teachers, police officers, and strangers.
2. Name or show a picture of each grown-up. Coach your child to nod or shake their head for each person.

NOTE: If you identify someone as a safe grown-up in your child's life, make sure that person knows you've identified them as a safe adult. You might talk with them about how you plan to handle different situations so everyone responds to your child in a similar way. For example, ask them to listen without judgment, reassure the child they did the right thing coming to you, and take appropriate action. Ask those safe adults to tell you every time something unsafe happens or any time your child comes to them for help so you are aware.

Who's Here to Help?

This activity is designed to help your child understand when to turn to a safe grown-up for help in different settings.

You want your child to understand who to go to in each situation and what to do if they tell a safe grown-up but the situation doesn't improve. Feel free to use the situations described here or add your own.

MATERIALS
· Paper
· Pencil or pen

INSTRUCTIONS
1. With your child, make a list of your child's safe grown-ups, including some generic safe adults (police, labeled helpers, etc.).
2. One at a time, describe different scenarios in a specific setting (see note following) and ask your child to tell you which safe grown-up(s) they can talk to in each situation.

NOTE: Here are some ideas to get you started:
· You're at your grandparents' home, and a stranger knocks on the door.
· You're at school, and another kid hits you.
· You're having a playdate at your home, and your friend asks to see your private parts.

- We're at the store, and you can't find me.
- You told your teacher that another kid pushed you. The next day, they push you again, but your teacher does not do anything about it.

Sometimes, children tell an adult about their safety concerns and that adult does not appear to help them. Perhaps the child is not communicating clearly or the adult thinks they took care of the problem but it didn't work. Teach your child to tell another adult if needed and to always let you know what happened.

Look for the Badge

The goal of this activity is to help your child recognize who they can go to in an emergency if you're not there or are unable to help them.

This is a real-life activity you can do when you're out in public, such as in stores, restaurants, parks, or anywhere else you frequent with your child.

INSTRUCTIONS

1. While out in different public places with your child, point out the helpers.
2. Tell your child how you figured out that person might be a helper (see note following).
3. Encourage your child to find the helpers. Praise them when they are able to do so on their own.

NOTE: Point out the clues that someone is a helper. It might be that they are wearing a uniform or name badge, they are behind the counter, they are greeting everyone, or they have children with them, too.

Is It Tattling?

It's important for children to understand that telling a safe adult about not-okay touches, things that make them uncomfortable, and other unsafe situations is not tattling. They should always tell a safe grown-up right away.

It can also be challenging for children to know what constitutes an unsafe situation versus a situation that does not need to be reported right away. In this activity, you'll introduce these nuances and start the conversation.

MATERIALS
· Paper
· Green crayon or marker

INSTRUCTIONS
1. Draw a green circle.
2. Ask your child to name things they should tell an adult right away that are not considered tattling (see note following).
3. Write down correct responses in the green circle. Write incorrect responses outside the circle, and discuss why those examples do not go in the green circle.

NOTE: If your child struggles with ideas, provide examples using the different okay and not-okay touches we've explored throughout the book. Offer praise when they get it right! It's typical for young children to struggle with tattling. To help them understand, discuss some of the tattling examples and explain that they can tell you anything, but that's not something they must tell you. If they come to you tattling, you might just say "okay" and change the subject—this will help them recognize what constitutes tattling and that it doesn't always get a response. You might also label tattling when it occurs so they understand it's not something they need to report right away.

CHAPTER 8

Distinguishing Between Privacy, Secrets, and Surprises

WE'VE EXPLORED HOW to talk with your child about private parts and why we use the word "private" to describe them. In this chapter, we talk about privacy. We can explain that privacy means we want to keep something to ourselves or within our family. Teaching your child about privacy will help them learn to respect boundaries for themselves and others and help them differentiate between times it's okay to be curious and when to stop inquiring.

WHY THIS, WHY NOW?

Children are naturally curious. Most of the time, we encourage and answer their questions (even if it's annoying to hear "Why?" for the 25th time). However, even a child's wonderful sense of curiosity needs boundaries. We don't share personal information with them just to answer their questions. Similarly, we teach them they don't have to tell everyone everything about themself or their family. You may have already corrected your child at some point for oversharing. Messages like this begin to teach them about privacy.

In some instances, children are asked to keep secrets. By helping them understand what secrets are, we can teach them when secrets are okay to keep and when they should be told. We'll also talk about two types of secrets: surprise secrets that make people happy, and scary secrets that hurt or scare people. Surprise secrets might include a secret handshake, a surprise party, Secret Santa gifts, and having a present for someone. Scary secrets include not telling when someone is hurting someone else, breaking rules or laws, and making threats toward others. We also want to set a precedent that they never have secrets from you.

Vocabulary

The terms "**surprise/happy secret**" and "**scary/hurting secret**" can help children differentiate and discern whether a secret is one they should keep or tell. Avoiding the terms "**good**" and "**bad**" around secrets keeps judgment out of the conversation. This way, children don't need to worry about being in trouble for something "bad."

CONVERSATION GUIDE

Use everyday moments to teach your child about privacy and the different types of secrets.

GETTING STARTED

These everyday moments will help your child understand the differences in secrets on a deeper level and enable more natural and meaningful conversations. For example, you might start teaching about privacy when you ask your child to stand outside the bathroom while you use the toilet or explain why we close the stalls in a public bathroom. Similarly, for secrets, teach them about surprise secrets when they help you pick out a gift for someone. Help them understand it won't be a secret for long and it will make the person happy. That's what makes it a surprise secret and an okay secret to keep. Teaching about scary secrets doesn't come as naturally. Discuss when it's not okay to keep something a secret, even if someone tells them to keep the secret, such as when a not-okay touch happens.

CONTINUING THE CONVERSATION

As your child gets older, use real-life opportunities to discuss privacy, such as when they overshare with a stranger or ask overly personal questions. Every family is different, so your views on privacy will center around your culture and family. Talk about what's acceptable and unacceptable in your family.

Children won't always follow our rules about privacy; we can use those instances as learning lessons. We don't want our children to feel as though they are in trouble; rather, we want them to learn the nuances of privacy and be reminded to think through potential consequences if they overshare with others. As the conversation continues around privacy, help your child understand more nuanced situations for secrets as well, such as when a friend tells them they have a crush on someone or something very personal.

SCRIPTS

Here are three scripts you can use to discuss privacy and secrets. Script 1 is geared toward a three-year-old, script 2 to a four- or five-year-old, and script 3 to a six-year-old. Feel free to adapt these to meet your child where they are.

SCRIPT 1: PRIVACY

Caregiver: I'm going to the bathroom, and I would like privacy. This means I want to be by myself and don't want to share my body or thoughts with someone else.
Child: I always come in!

Caregiver: Now that you're older and using the potty yourself, I would like privacy, which means you can't come into the bathroom with me anymore. It's okay if you wait outside the door or go play with your toys.

Child: But you come in with me.

Caregiver: That's true, and you're right. Now that you can go potty yourself, you can have privacy while you go, too. I'll be out in a minute when I'm finished (the caregiver goes into the bathroom and locks the door).

Child: (Waits outside the bathroom.)

Caregiver (comes out of the bathroom): Thank you for giving me privacy!

SCRIPT 2: SURPRISE VERSUS SCARY SECRETS

Child: I have a secret!

Caregiver: What is it? We don't have secrets from each other because I'm your caregiver.

Child: Aunt Nancy and I did something together at the party, and she said we should keep it a secret.

Caregiver: Hmm, secrets from me are not safe. Is it a surprise secret or a scary secret?

Child: I don't know.

Caregiver: Well, did you and Aunt Nancy do something that made you and her happy and safe, or did it hurt or make you or her scared?

Child: Oh, it was happy! So happy!

Caregiver: Okay, then it's a surprise secret and not a scary secret.

Child: Oh, yes! You are going to be happy and surprised!

Caregiver: That's good to hear. Would you like to tell [other caregiver] or me what the secret is?

Child: Okay, I'll tell you now. Look (holds up drawing)! We drew you a picture. Surprise!

Caregiver: Thank you! This is a great surprise! It was a surprise secret and okay to keep. I'm still happy you shared it with me. I want to know your secrets so I can help you figure out whether they are surprise secrets or scary secrets. Okay?

Child: Okay.

SCRIPT 3: TELLING SCARY SECRETS

Caregiver: Some people who hurt other people tell them to keep it a secret. They don't want to get in trouble, so they want it to be a secret. But if they do something wrong, the other person is hurt and scared. When we are hurt and scared, we need help. Who can help you if someone hurts you?

Child: You! And Mommy, Grandma, Grandpa, Ms. Heather.

Caregiver: That's right. Those are your safe grown-ups. You can tell them anything. I want to make sure you always tell us if something scary or hurtful happens so we can help you.

Child: Oh, I will!

Caregiver: Good. If a person hurts or scares you and tells you to keep it a secret, what should you do?

Child: Tell you anyway. That's a scary secret.

Caregiver: Exactly! And you can tell me all of your secrets.

Child: I need to tell you a secret.

Caregiver: What?

Child: I ate bubble gum yesterday, and I swallowed it.

Caregiver: Thanks for being honest. I'm glad you told me.

Child: Am I going to get hurt?

Caregiver: No, I think your body can handle it, but don't do it again. Your body doesn't like it. I'm glad you told me.

Child: Okay.

ACTIVITIES

Here are four activities you can weave into your interactions with your child to help teach and reinforce information about privacy and secrets. You might pick one activity to do now, and do additional activities as your child gets older, or repeat activities as you'd like, making them more age appropriate as your child grows.

Tell Me a Secret

Review what a secret is with your child. Remind them they can tell you everything and should never keep scary secrets from you.

Explain to your child that, sometimes, people whisper secrets into another person's ear as a way to keep the information private—just like you'll do in this activity.

INSTRUCTIONS

1. Tell your child you're going to pretend to tell each other secrets.
2. Whisper a statement like, "I love when you give me hugs," into their ear.
3. Invite your child to whisper something into your ear.
4. Take turns telling "secrets."
5. Praise your child for sharing information with you, and tell them how happy it makes you when they tell you everything.

NOTE: It's expected that every caregiver will have secrets from their children, especially when the children are young. This makes sense. After all, children don't need to carry the burden of knowing all their caregivers' private business—they'll be dealing with their own adult issues one day soon enough! When talking with your child about the importance of not keeping secrets from you, resist any urge to say you have secrets or promise you will not keep secrets from your child. Instead, explain that while adults can care for themselves, children need protection—that's why it's important for them to share secrets with you.

Scary or Surprise?

When is it safe to keep a secret, and when is it not safe?

Knowing the difference between types of secrets is an important skill for children to learn for their safety. This activity makes it fun to talk about. It's okay to laugh as you discuss these hard topics because your child will become more comfortable and likely to talk to you about secrets in the future.

INSTRUCTIONS

1. Explain to your child that you are going to name different secrets and you want them to make a surprise face if it's a surprise secret or a scary face if it's a scary secret.
2. Name each secret, and praise your child when they make the correct face.

NOTE: Try these examples, or make up your own:

- You bought someone a present.
- You had a secret handshake.
- Someone touched your private parts.
- Someone hit you.
- Someone told you who they like.
- Someone is having a surprise party.
- Someone showed you their private parts.
- Someone tickled you and made you uncomfortable.
- You made a craft to give someone.

When to Keep, When to Tell

This activity reviews surprise secrets versus scary secrets. It'll remind your child they should always tell a safe grown-up if a scary secret happens.

The more you practice the actions and words your child can use when a safety issue arises, the more prepared they will be. Repetition helps them know what to do instead of freezing if they get scared.

INSTRUCTIONS

1. Tell your child you're going to practice what to do if someone tells them to keep a secret.
2. Tell them you're pretending to be a grown-up at school. Say, "We're going to make a craft for your parents. Don't tell them, okay?"
3. Prompt your child to respond. They may say, "Okay. I can't wait to give it to them!"
4. Now, tell them you're pretending to be that grown-up again and say, "Come into the bathroom. I want to show you something in my pants."
5. Prompt your child to respond. Coach them if needed to use "Stop, Go, Tell" (see page 62), telling another safe adult at school. Then, have them pretend to come home and tell you about it.

NOTE: Reassure your child that it was so good they told you the scary secret, and praise them for being brave. By hearing your reassuring response, your child will be much more likely to tell you scary secrets in the future. They'll understand you are going to be supportive and kind and not upset with them in any way. Sometimes, children worry about telling their safe adults secrets because they don't know how they will respond and are afraid of getting in trouble. This activity reinforces that the child did nothing wrong and assures that future conversations of this kind will go well.

Look How Far You've Come!

Children can surprise us with all the information they retain.

This final activity uses a fun game to see what your child has learned about privacy, secrets, and surprises. Prepare some questions in advance, and let them move forward to victory!

MATERIALS
- 5 or 6 pieces of paper
- Marker (optional)

INSTRUCTIONS
1. Lay the papers across the floor so your child can step from one to the next. Invite them to stand on the first piece of paper.
2. Ask a question about privacy or secrets (see note following). If they get the answer right, let them move forward one paper. If they get it wrong, they don't move.
3. Ask questions until your child reaches the last paper. Reward them with praise and a loving okay touch!

NOTE: Here are some ideas to get you started:
- What is something you need privacy for?
- When should you tell a secret to a safe grown-up?
- Who should you tell a scary secret to?
- Can you tell me a secret you have?
- Can you think of a surprise secret?
- What should you do if a grown-up doesn't help you with your secret?

If they get an answer wrong, offer a quick explanation so they understand the right answer. Depending on age and comprehension level, increase or decrease the difficulty of the questions. Feel free to number the papers (such as one through five) to illustrate their progress—and reinforce their counting skills!

Conclusion

Congratulations on working through this book, and kudos for teaching your child invaluable skills related to body safety and boundaries. Even at this young age, you have taught them so much, including:

- How to listen to their body's clues and understand their feelings
- How to respect other people's personal space and boundaries
- How to identify and assert their own preferences regarding personal space and boundaries
- The proper names of private parts
- The differences between okay and not-okay touches
- What to do if someone tries to give them a not-okay touch
- Who their safe adults are
- How to identify and approach helpers when they don't know anyone
- The importance of privacy and respect for others' privacy
- The differences between surprise and scary secrets and what to do about each

Please revisit this book as often as needed and review the conversations and activities with your child. Repetition will help this information stick. As your child grows, adapt your conversations and the content of each activity to include new age-appropriate concepts. This discussion, along with many others, will continue throughout their childhood. Your child is off to a great start, thanks to you!

Resources

Additional books you may find helpful:

Do You Have a Secret?
by Jennifer Moore-Mallinos
This book helps children understand the different types of secrets and when to tell a secret to an adult.

I Said No! A Kid-To-Kid Guide to Keeping Private Parts Private
by Zack and Kimberly King
This book helps children understand what to do if someone tries to look at or touch their private parts by telling the story of a boy who went to a sleepover, where the other child tried to be inappropriate.

No Means No!
by Jayneen Sanders
This book helps children understand it is okay to say no sometimes and how to do that with others.

Personal Space Camp
by Julia Cook
This book helps children understand that everyone has personal space we need to respect.

The Mouse, The Monster, and Me: Assertiveness for Young People
by Pat Palmer, EdD
This book for school-age children helps them learn how to be assertive instead of passive or aggressive.

Additional videos and websites you might find helpful:

"Consent for Kids"
youtu.be/h3nhM9UlJjc
This video teaches children about consent.

Consent Parenting
www.consentparenting.com/blog
Blog and related resources teaching children about body safety, boundaries, and consent.

Emotional Well-Bring
https://sesameworkshop.org/topics/mentalhealth/
Various videos on feeling and coping and on raising children who are healthy in mind, body, and heart

Index

Acknowledgments

I must first express gratitude to my husband, Keith, and my parents, Dan and Nancy Tiemeier, for helping me pursue a lifelong bucket list item. Without you caring for our children, I would not have had the space to write this book. I'm also humbled by the support and patience of my children, Audrey, Samantha, and Ryland, as I took time away from you to write. Thank you to my village of family and friends who helped me reach this point, personally and professionally. I am blessed with each of you.

To my educators, supervisors, and colleagues, thank you for laying the foundation for this material and for your inspiration. Dr. Mike Nelson, Dr. Barbara Boat, Dr. Erica Messer, Dr. Dawn Blacker, Dr. Georganna Sedlar, Dr. Julie Lippman, Dr. Esther Deblinger and many others have afforded me the knowledge, vision, and sophistication to provide a great service to my patients and their families. Dr. Heather Bensman, Dr. Megan Radenhausen, and Dr. Nicole Zahka, I am immensely grateful for your consultations and genuine friendship.

Lastly, a very special thank you to the team at Zeitgeist Publishing for guiding me through writing my first book.

About the Author

 **Dr. Julie Bemerer** is a clinical psychologist from Cincinnati, Ohio. Dr. Bemerer specializes in working with trauma-affected youth and their families. She provides state-of-the art treatment to children of all ages for post-traumatic stress symptoms.

Dr. Bemerer completed her undergraduate education at Miami University of Ohio and her graduate education at Xavier University. She completed her predoctoral internship at the UC Davis CAARE Diagnostic and Treatment Center in Sacramento, California, and her postdoctoral fellowship at the Rowan Medicine CARES Institute in Stratford, New Jersey. She practices at Cincinnati Children's Hospital Medical Center. Dr. Bemerer is married with three children and enjoys traveling.

Hi there,

We hope *The Body Boundaries Parenting Guide* helped you.
If you have any questions or concerns about your
book, or have received a damaged copy, please contact
customerservice@penguinrandomhouse.com. We're here
and happy to help.

Also, please consider writing a review on your favorite
retailer's website to let others know what you thought
of the book.

Sincerely,

The Zeitgeist Team